FLIN[T]

MW01717569

A practical guide

Jonathan Cope

The author reaching out across history in one of the side caverns at Grimes Graves, a Neolithic flint mine in Norfolk, UK. I'm reaching out to (but not touching) an original flint mining pick made from red deer antler, last used thousands of years ago! You can see the 'floor' flint that the miners were extracting directly behind me.

Design and layout by J. Cope

Published by Sound For Health / Jonathan Cope
www.soundforhealth.com
email: jonnycope@hotmail.com

©2023 Jonathan Cope. All text, photographs and illustrations.
The right of Jonathan Cope to be identified as the Author of this work has been asserted in accordance with the Copyright, Designs and Patents Act 1988.

All rights reserved. No part of this publication may reproduced, stored in a retrieval system, or transmitted, in any form or by any means, without the prior written permission of the publisher, nor be otherwise circulated in any form of binding other than that in which it is published and without similar condition being imposed on the subsequent purchaser.

ISBN 979 0 9539 8114 4

CONTENTS

INTRODUCTION

One of the most ancient craft skills, flint knapping has been important for almost all of human existence. Flint (chert) is a form of quartz, or silicon dioxide, also known as silica (silex). It occurs in layers and irregular nodules in chalk and some other limestones. It is widely found around the world and was a primary material in the production of stone age tools and weapons.

Flint, and the chalk deposits that often host it, were formed millions of years ago. They were created by the laying down of thick layers of organic material, the remains of billions of sea creatures. Over time these layers became compressed and underwent complex chemical processes. The silica contained in the debris was changed over eons into the substance we now know as flint. It tends to form distinct bands within the chalky layers that carry it. It can be found in the Southern and Eastern parts of England and has similar forms throughout the world. Flint is very hard, 7 on the Mohr scale, with diamonds at 10.

There are many ways to approach flint knapping and many disciplines or interests will lead to an awareness of it; archaeology, ancient history, anthropology, bushcraft and 'survival' skills, etc. It is, quite obviously, a manual skill and is best learnt through direct experience and practice. However, such experience can prove hard to come by so I hope the guidance included in this book will go some way to help you on your journey. Knapping can sometimes be frustrating but is ultimately a very rewarding skill. Whatever piqued your interest in this subject you will certainly gain insights and appreciation for the skills used by our ancient ancestors to make tools and weapons that aided their survival.

The aim of this book is to give solid grounding in the practical aspects of this ancient craft. I have assumed no knowledge on behalf of the reader but those with any experience should still find plenty to help them on their knapping journey. I will touch on some historical aspects and tool types but will not make a complete classification of the myriad tools that exist within the archaeological record. Please see the resources section at the end of the book for further reading.

FLINT AND SIMILAR, KNAPPABLE, MATERIALS

Flint. As stated previously, flint is a silica-rich material that can have a predictable pattern of breakage when subject to stress (hitting). This allows it to be shaped into useful tools. The best flint has a glossy black appearance.

Chert. A fine-grained sedimentary rock with microcrystalline grains of quartz. It can be knapped in much the same way as flint.

Obsidian. An igneous rock and naturally occurring 'glass' formed during volcanic eruptions. It is extremely (microscopically) fine grained. When knapped it produces some of the sharpest edges found in nature and can slice between molecules! It is not found in the UK (sadly).

Glass and ceramic. Glass shares much of its make-up (silica) with flint and can be knapped using similar methods to flint. Obviously, it is more abundant than other natural materials and is a good choice if access to flint is limited. Some ceramics can also be knapped successfully.

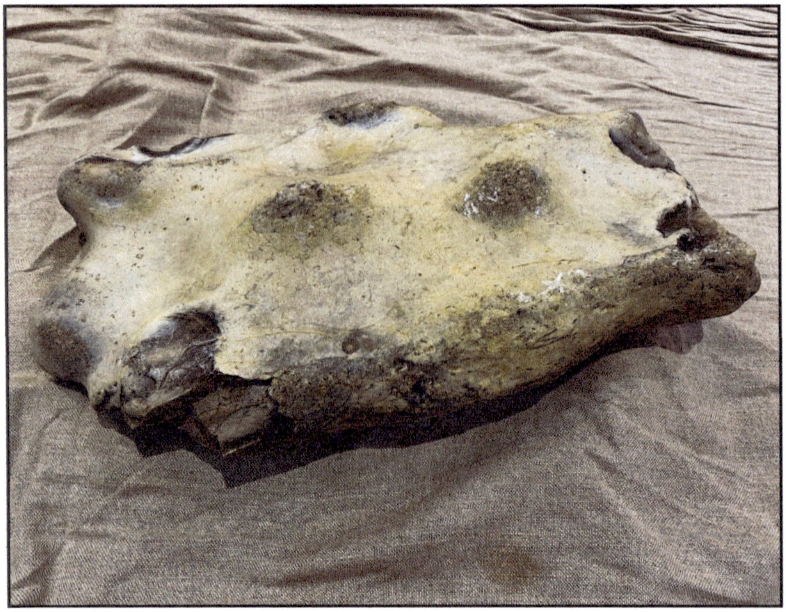

1. Flint nodule.

TERMINOLOGY

It can be helpful to understand many of the terms used in the following text, as some may not be obvious or are even a little obscure.

Abrasion. Using a gritty material to abrade or dull sharp edges prior to striking, or for safety.

Abrupt flakes. A flake that is quite short and doesn't travel far from the point of impact.

Biface. An edged tool with both edges sharpened, usually of convex section like a lentil.

Blade. A detached flake with parallel sides, more often longer than its own width.

Bulb of percussion. The bulge created on the 'inside' (ventral) side of a struck flake. This is part of the cone radiating out from the impact point.

Chaîne opératoire. French for 'chain of operation' – the order of a process like flint knapping.

Conchoidal fracture. 'Shell-like' – used to describe the smooth fracturing seen in materials like flint and glass.

Core. A piece of flint that has had flakes removed from it.

Cortical flake. A flint flake with remains of cortex on its dorsal side.

Cortex. The outside coating on a flint nodule that consists of chalky deposits.

Crested blade. A ridge found along the length of blades with previous removals.

Debitage. Waste material, including flakes, produced during the knapping process.

Direct percussion. Hitting the flint directly with hard or soft hammers.

Distal end. The opposite end to the one that is struck.

Dorsal surface. The 'outside' surface of a flake and which often carries scars of previous removals.

End shock. A catastrophic break, usually across the width of a stone tool, often caused by incorrect platform preparation, but can also be the product of interior inclusions within the flint.

Fissures. Fractures or stress lines that radiate away from the point of impact.

Facets. The 'flat' surfaces left behind after a flake is removed.

Flake. A piece of material removed by striking or pressure.

Flake scars. Previous flake removals.

Hafting. The fitting of a 'handle' to a stone tool.

Hertzian cone. The conical wavefront that passes through certain materials when impacted.

Indirect percussion. Using another implement when striking flint, often an antler punch that is hit with a soft hammer.

Invasive flakes. Flake removal that travels a long way into / across the material.

Isolation. Preparing a striking platform by abrading either side of it.

Knapper. Someone who creates stone tools by impact / pressure.

Knapping. The process of creating tools by impact / pressure.

Microliths. Very small flint tools, mainly created in the Mesolithic (Middle Stone Age).

Nodule. A naturally occurring lump of flint.

Patina. The surface colours that occur on older flint.

Platform. An area that is struck with a hammer to detach a flake.

Preform. A partially finished stone tool.

Proximal end. The struck end of a flake that carries the bulb of percussion / platform.

Radial ridges. Ridges that sit at 90 degrees to the bulb of percussion and that appear as 'ripples' across the ventral side of a struck flake.

Retouch. Further work on a struck edge to change its profile.

Reduction. The process of removing material via knapping to produce tools.

Rough-out. As per Preform.

Shock waves. The propagation (spreading out) of forces like the impact of hammer on flint.

Silicon. A non-metallic element that exists in practically all rocks and sands, earth, etc.

Striking platform. An area (prepared or not) that will take impact to create a flake.

Thinning. The process of flake removal to create tools.

Ventral surface. The 'inside' of a flake that carries the bulb of percussion.

SELECTING MATERIAL

This can be the biggest hurdle for any beginning knapper as materials can be surprisingly hard to find. Geology plays an important role here and you may be lucky to live in a flint-bearing area, or not. Wherever you find your flint, it pays to 'trial knap' right then and there if you can. There is little point carrying off pieces that will be of no use, because of damage or other factors. When held lightly in the hand and gently struck with a suitable hammerstone, good flint will 'ring' with an almost bell-like tone. Discard anything that produces a 'clunk' or dull sound. Flint is a natural product so is found in a wide range of shapes and sizes. As we will lose anything up to 80% of the volume of a nodule in the knapping process, it pays to select nodules of at least large orange size and preferably more like rugby ball size. Anything too spherical is difficult to deal with and too flat / thin will be of little use. Try to aim for 'lenticular' or lens shapes – double convex or 'bulged out'.

Flint very often has crevices, holes and inclusions of other material like quartz, small fossils, etc. All of these will make knapping more difficult so select carefully. Be aware that, when beginning to knap, you will quickly use up quite a quantity of material as you learn how it reacts. It can take many nodules and many, many hours to gain even basic skills. Use your material sparingly unless you are in the lucky situation of having an abundance on your doorstep. Trial knapping will quickly demonstrate the likely quality in any given area. The ideal is a nice, even, dark bluey-black colour with few inclusions. The really good stuff will knap smoothly, is almost glass-like in appearance, and flakes will display all the components we need to look for – bulb of percussion, ripples, etc.

Field flint

Please do not head straight out into local fields without first obtaining permission from the landowner. Ask around, or use Google, to discover who your local farmers / landowners are and approach them with a polite request. As flint nodules can damage expensive agricultural machinery, most farmers will be only too happy to have you remove large nodules for them! Once permission is obtained be sure to be clear about where you are allowed to go, access points, etc. Most farmers will not want you wandering over their crops. This may limit potential searching to times of the year when fields are freshly ploughed, namely Spring and Autumn in the UK. Field flint can vary greatly in quality, from black and almost glass-like, to more grainy types that can be grey or light brown. Nodules found in ploughed fields are likely to have damage caused by impacts from machinery and weather. Avoid any with more severe damage. Also look out for 'crazing' in the surface. If water gets into cracks in flint it can freeze in cold weather, and this can rapidly cause much internal damage to the flint. This can be hard to see from the outside but makes itself known when a struck nodule 'explodes' into little bits at the first strike. Better to just leave it where it is.

2. Typical field flint nodule.

A side note. If you are searching for flint in ploughed fields, you may be searching in areas used by our ancestors. Keep a look out for anything that displays the tell-tale signs of human working. (You will know after reading this book or starting to knap yourself). You may well discover actual ancient artefacts. You may gain great insights by studying actual ancient examples of knapped flint, both finished tools and 'waste' flakes.

Beach flint

If you are within easy access of the southern coast on England, you might consider searching along beaches for your materials. It might seem obvious to many, but flint will only be found in areas near chalk deposits, so you are unlikely to find much on sandy beaches. Pebble beaches are much more productive. Although beaches are also subject to land ownership there is often a more acceptable grey area in terms of access and use. Obviously, we cannot expect to walk off a beach with great armfuls of material, but a few select nodules seems acceptable in most situations. Beach flint has some added benefits, namely the cortex is often completely removed by erosion and the nodules become more rounded.

3. Great pebble beach.

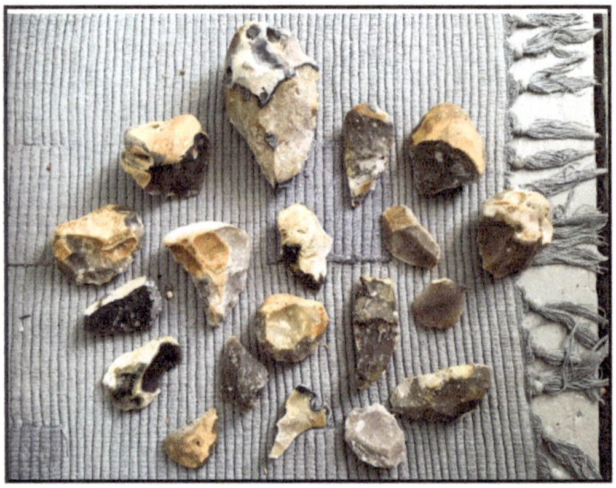

4. Holiday beach knapping.

If you follow my advice of test knapping, please be mindful that beaches are more 'public' spaces. Take any nodules you wish to check away from the crowds and dispose of any sharp flakes produced. Either take them with you (they may be useful) or cast them well out into the sea. Alternatively, I sometimes dig a hole in the pebbles and bury any flakes, so they are out of harm's way. I have spent several holidays sat on pebble beaches working at furthering my knapping skills. I take home anything I'm pleased with and discard the mistakes and waste by digging a pit and safely depositing it all under at least 30cm of pebbles. You may also find nodules in river and stream beds, and some random scatters literally anywhere, if ancient glacial action has carried and deposited flint (and other material) from elsewhere.

Pic 4. shows a morning's work whilst on holiday. As can be seen, most of this material is a more grainy chert type. This material was more suited to 'earlier' type tools; top right has a couple of 'Oldawan' style choppers, top centre is a more 'Acheulian' hand axe, with the rest a mix of flakes, scrapers, backed knives, a spear point roughout, borer, etc. Much experience and insight can be gained from this type of working.

Quarried / tabular flint

The 'holy grail' for most knappers is freshly quarried flint. It should be no surprise that our ancient ancestors also realised this fact and went to great lengths to dig good flint from seams under the ground. An amazing ancient flint mining site can be found at Grimes Graves, near Thetford in Norfolk. Flint is considered a by-product of most modern quarrying, which is usually for limestone or chalk so many quarries sell or even discard it. This type of flint must only be acquired by contacting the quarry owners and arranging to go and buy some. They may have nodules in size order or just a random pile. Agree prices, often by weight, and try to test sample pieces if possible.

Flint suppliers

You may find flint nodules via building merchants. These are usually smaller nodules used in construction and the facing of walls. It will be offered either as part knapped or unknapped. As you can rarely select it yourself, I would suggest opting for the unknapped varieties. Be aware that the material can vary quite a bit so do not expect all nodules to be of ideal shape and size, or even quality. This can be an expensive option but may be necessary if you live in certain areas of the country. Most suppliers will deliver. Obtain trial pieces whenever possible, before investing in any quantity.

Glass

If flint proves difficult to obtain then you can learn several of the key skills by using glass as an alternative. It seems a good 'eco' choice, but we actually can't just use any glass. Most will be too thin to be of any use. All flint knapping is a reduction process, with end products much smaller and

thinner than the starting piece. You can try enquiries at glazing firms as they may have off-cuts of thicker glass. Avoid tempered / safety glass as it has layers of plastic inside that render it useless for our purposes.
A sensible thickness of glass can be found in a surprising place – the bottoms of beer bottles! More on this later.

Ceramics

Some thicker, fine grained, types of ceramic can be knapped. White earthenware, as used to make sinks and toilets works surprisingly well and is of usable thickness for reduction. Scrap yards or reclamation sites are the obvious places to source these. Butlers sinks (for example) have a very solid thickness and can be worked via all methods; direct, indirect and pressure. Thick floor tiles and other similar thicker sectioned ceramic material may also be a great place to gain lots of practice, saving the expense or difficulty of sourcing quality flint. Most tile supply shops may have old or broken stock they would be willing to part with. Most ceramic is substanially softer than flint so will knap with less force and is easy to break by over doing it.

Some people have joked that, should society face some future collapse, being able to knap tools and weapons from broken sanitary ware might become the 'Space Age Stone Age'.

5. Glass bottle bottom.

6. Thick ceramic tile.

TOOLS

Very little is needed to start basic knapping – almost just a beach pebble but to progress and to be safe some extra equipment is useful. Start with the basics and add more as your knapping skills progress.

Hard hammers

Hard hammers are just that – any stone hard enough to take the impact. Common choices are quartzite pebbles or sandstone. Try to find nice round pebbles that fit well in the hand. Egg shaped can be very useful too. A selection, ranging from fist-sized (or larger), to egg-sized will give good flexibility. It is common for hammerstones to break, especially when a beginner, so collect at least five or six. Avoid any with damage. You will typically find these types of pebbles on most rocky beaches and almost always where you are finding flint. I have a preference for smooth brown

7. A selection of hard and soft hammers, along with some pressure flaking tools and some abrading stones.

‘beach’ pebbles. Alternatively, you can also find these types of pebbles at many building suppliers / DIY centres.

Soft hammers

The obvious choice for soft hammers is deer antler. It has an amazing blend of strength and flexibility and is ideal for knapping. Our ancestors used it for a reason. Pretty much any antler will work, but as you progress you will find that you may need a range of sizes and weights and that some species are more useful than others. Antler is perfect for this work as, although very tough and quite hard, it will ‘give’ a little when used to strike flint. This both absorbs shock and lends a more ‘whip-like’ motion to the strike. The rounded end sections sort of ‘grab’ the edge of the flint, which helps start the flake removal shockwave.

Look online (see resource section) for antler hammers or make your own. If you are lucky enough to live somewhere frequented by deer, you could try looking for shed antlers. Stags grow, then shed, antlers throughout their lives so if you can walk through the type of woodland they pass through you may be fortunate enough to find sheds. Most species of UK deer antler will work but my preference is for Red Deer as it is the densest, and stags can grow antlers of considerable weight and size.

A side note here; unfortunately for us there has been a huge rise in the use of antler for dog chews and this has led to a very noticeable shortage and inflated prices. You may be able to exploit this, however, and buy

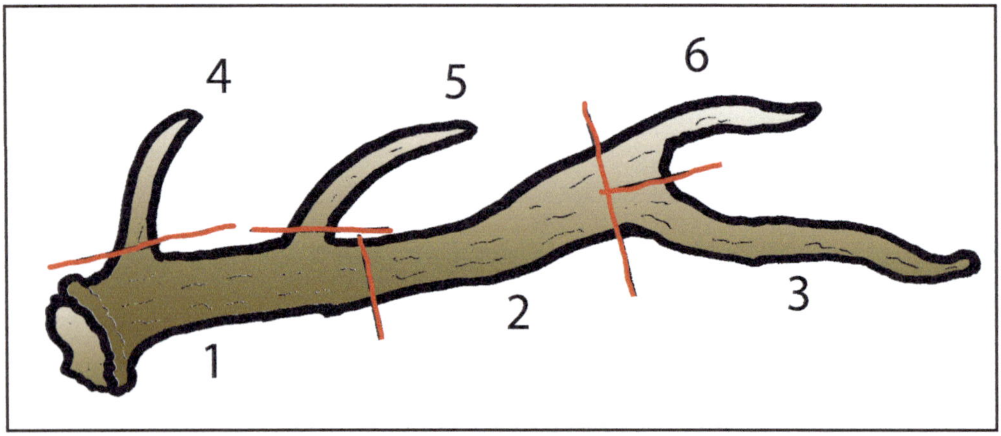

8. Antler sections for soft hammers / pressure flakers

sections destined for chews and use them for knapping tools. Try to find longer and heavier chunks.

My personal preference is to try to obtain a complete antler as this can be cut into many useful sections. Antler cuts quite easily with a hacksaw and a rough file or rasp will help smooth and shape the sections. If you do use power tools, be aware that the heat produced will create quite a smell, think burnt hair!

Here are some suggestions for a basic 'tool kit', see picture 8.

Use the crown end for a heavy hammer. Aim for around 20-30cm length. Round off both ends with files (1).

If long enough the next section after the crown end can produce a mid-weight hammer. Again, round off both ends. (2).

Moving towards the more pointed 'tines' you will be able to create lighter hammers that are ideal for thinning flakes. (3).

Lastly the tines themselves are perfect for use as pressure flakers. Leave the pointed end as it is but round off the cut end. 12-20cm is ideal for this use. (4, 5 & 6).

You can create a more modern version pressure flaker by drilling into the pointed end of a tine and inserting a rod of copper or bronze. This will last much longer than raw antler and can produce very precise flaking.

Punches for indirect percussion can be also created from antler (some hardwoods are also practical). Straighter sections of antler can be cut to around 15-20cm length. Use tools or sandpaper to round off both ends, with the thicker end slightly flatter and the thinner end slightly more pointed.

Abrading materials

Any abrasive stone will work – granite, sandstone, etc. Many modern knappers use broken sections of old abrasive grind wheels. These are made from silicon carbide and are very tough. A selection of sizes and shapes can be useful.

Leather pads

As we will be striking flakes from flint that is supported on our leg it will be necessary to protect ourselves from the very sharp flakes that result, along with dispersing some of the forces used when striking. Leather is very useful for guarding against cuts from sharp flint. The thicker the better, although it can prove to be trickier to get hold of leather much thicker than 2mm. You can of course, double over thinner leather. I prefer leather of at least 3-4mm. This can be further padded underneath with any folded material. I like to use sections of old carpet as it absorbs impacts well and is very cheap / free. We will need to use pads of leather large enough to protect the leg. A4 (paper size) or 21 x 29cm is a good size and allows the pad to wrap over the thigh for better protection. A more advanced version can be made by adding straps and a buckle that hold the pad in place around the leg.

Gloves

These should strike a balance between protection and practical use. Very thick leather gloves are great for protection but make handling more difficult. Thin cotton gloves offer little to no protection. Modern rubberised

9. Leather pads; carpet off-cut, folded leather, and a larger leg pad with buckle fitted.

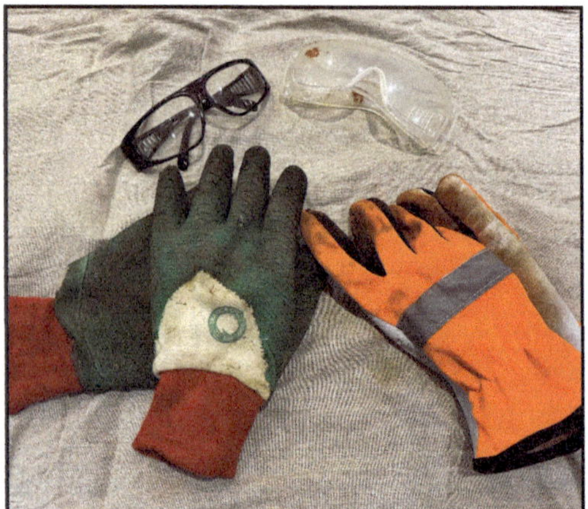

10. Types of goggles and work gloves.

'work' gloves, or thinner leather are ideal and not too expensive.

Goggles

If you wear glasses, you may elect to not use goggles. One word of caution; flakes are often detached with some force and can literally fly around. It's amazing how smaller pieces can fly upwards and even find their way between glasses and face, so goggles are a sensible precaution. If you don't wear glasses, you must wear safety glasses or goggles. Aim for clear plastic glasses, often made from polycarbonate. These should be a close fit to the face for the reasons stated above. You may elect to use goggles with sides and elastic. These offer excellent protection but do impact on vision slightly, especially peripheral vision. Make sure they have good ventilation otherwise they may just steam up and be unusable.

SAFETY WARNINGS

Warning: working with flint or glass is dangerous and should not be attempted by anyone under 16 without supervision. Knapping will produce very sharp flakes and dust. Always wear goggles or glasses, thick gloves and knap outdoors where possible due to fine dust. Flint knapping produces fine silica dust, which is very harmful to the lungs, so we must avoid inhaling it at all costs. Knapping outdoors will provide natural airflow to ensure that the dust is taken away from the knapper. If you must knap indoors, you will need dust extraction and / or a dust mask. Please ensure you wear solid, closed toe boots like walking boots – no wellies or trainers, and full-length trousers – jeans are ideal. When knapping, you must regularly brush off any flakes that collect around or under the piece you are working on. Impacts from knapping can drive even small flakes right through thick leather! Make sure flakes do not lodge in clothing folds or land in shoes, this is why higher boots are better. When you've finished make sure to brush yourself off carefully (with gloved hands) and even use a hoover to remove any fine dust. Do not shake off your clothing indoors!

Whether working outdoors or indoors please consider what will happen to all your debitage (waste). Cleaning up thousands of tiny sharp fragments is next to impossible and represents quite a hazard if left behind, so you may consider laying down a sheet or tarp. Make it large enough to cover the whole area where you are sitting. Two meters square is a good start. When you have finished it is much easier to gather up the tarp and tip all the contents into a bucket. Be sure to dispose of any unwanted waste in a considerate manner. Small amounts may be OK in domestic waste if double bagged. Dispose of as you would glass shards. Larger quantities may need burial in a small pit.

REDUCING LARGE NODULES

As many flint nodules are found with irregular shapes, basic reduction to achieve a more usable shape is a necessity. The nodule may also be too large to sensibly carry away from its findspot. Reducing nodules will be greatly affected by the type of material and how much cortex remains. If a nodule is covered in deep cortex (chalk) it will prove harder to 'get into'. If there are damaged areas, as often happens through natural or man-made processes, use these to gain access to the interior of the nodule. If there are few such areas, we can use the overall shape of the nodule to help us. If the cortex is very thick you can use a screwdriver to push and pry off the thicker chunks. The process of reducing down a large nodule into a sensible shape and size is known as 'quartering'. Obviously once you have done this you may wish to retain the smaller sections too if of useful size and shape. Whether you are sourcing your flint in field, beach,

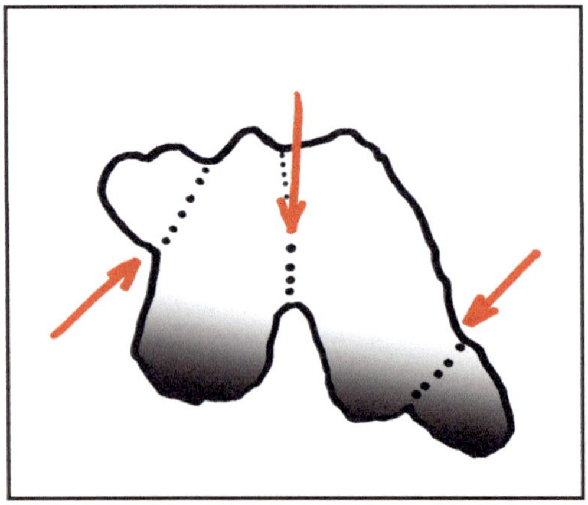

11. Quartering a larger nodule. Choices for impacts to remove chunks.

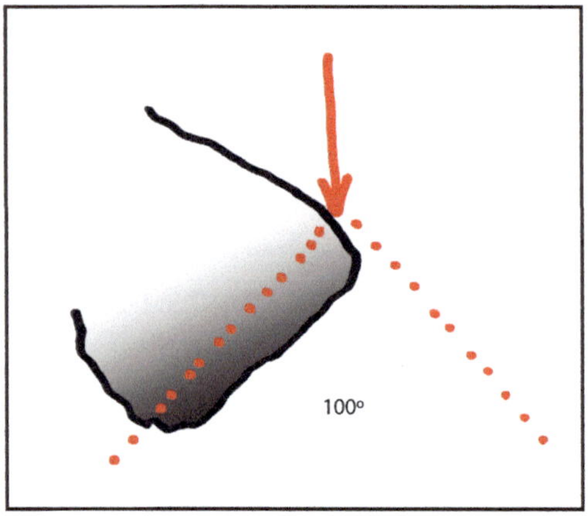

12.Hertzian cone shockwave travelling through flint.

or quarry this is a useful skill as it allows easier removal of oddly shaped nodules. We are nearly ready to start knapping but first some basic theory to consider.

Flint, and other silica rich materials, behave in reasonably predictable ways when exposed to stresses. Flint knapping is a reductive process – we remove material, either to use the resulting flakes as tools themselves, or to remove flakes and shape a nodule into a tool that is much smaller than the 'parent' nodule. The easiest way to get flint to flake off is to hit it. Basically, when you hit flint, a shockwave radiates out rapidly in an expanding cone shape. If the material is homogenous, that is, devoid of intrusions (other stuff), this shockwave will travel throughout the material until its momentum dissipates. We can use any hard stone, but quartzite pebbles work particularly well. These types of pebbles occur in the chalky layers and limestone deposits that also carry flint, so where you find one you will usually find the other.

In practice it is not desirable to hit directly into a 'face' of flint to achieve a full cone shockwave. This will cause a conical shockwave to travel inside the flint and is unproductive as it will not detach any flakes. This internal damage would only be revealed later if knapping work encroaches into any areas of damage. This kind of discovery can often happen when knapping, as this type of damage may have been caused by natural impacts as the flint rolled around in a field, or on a beach. What we will usually do, in most knapping, is hit an edge and control a partial 'cone' – a shockwave which will travel through the flint and, hopefully, cause a flake to detach. This shockwave, under the right conditions, will travel outwards at an angle of around 100 degrees, i.e. 50 degrees each side of the impact point (see picture 12). Knapping is all about learning the skill to control these impacts and detach flakes to create the desired shape(s).

STARTING OUT

Once you have sourced some flint you should go ahead and try knapping it. Although some knowledge of the basic theory can be useful, there is no substitute for actual practice. You may well learn more in a couple of practical sessions than in reading chunks of this book over and over. Note: All my descriptions of practical knapping (and pictures) assume a right-handed person. I apologise for this bias. Simply mirror instructions if you are left-handed. When knapping, even with care, small cuts are quite common so keep some finger plasters handy. Flint cuts are mainly quite superficial but can bleed quite profusely! Any cuts are often so 'clean' that they will heal quickly without issue but deal with any as soon as you notice them. I have often been absorbed in my knapping and find myself wondering where the red stuff on my nodule is coming from. As you gain more confidence and skill in knapping, and handling your work, cuts will happen less frequently. Without being alarmist, if you have any type of blood-clotting issue (Haemophilia) then flint knapping may not be for you.

Seated outdoors with all the appropriate safety gear and tools? Let's try to knap some flint. Read the following and see pictures 13 - 18.

Place the leather pad on your left leg, just above the knee. Take your flint and, using your left hand, hold it down onto the leather pad. Angle the flint towards you so that you can see the area that you will strike with the hammerstone. The strike area should overhang the inside of your thigh. The aim is for the struck piece to fall off onto the floor and for as little of the shock of the strike to connect with your leg as possible. Bruises are all part of the learning process but can be avoided as your skills improve.

Take up the hammerstone in your right hand. Hold it with your fingertips, not in the palm of your hand. Many knappers place their index finger on top of the hammerstone to help aim their strike. Gently place the stone on

13. Nodule on knee pad, hammerstone in hand

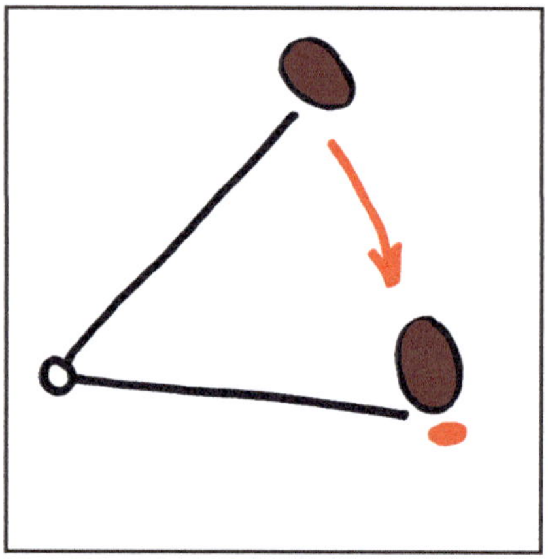

14. Smooth arc from 1 - 3 °clock

the flint to gauge your strike. You are aiming to contact the flint approximately 4 - 10mm in from the edge. Less and the edge will just crush and collapse, no flake will detach. More and the flake will either be too large, or you will just cause internal damage to the flint that will severely hamper further striking in that area.

Try to keep the right elbow in contact with the body and raise the hand / arm to about a 1 o'clock position. The strike area will be sitting at the 3 o'clock position. Your hand should make a smooth arc going down and your elbow should not move away from your body. Think of your elbow as a hinge and make sure your forearm moves in a smooth arc between the two points. Your wrist or fingers should not flex as this will change the arc of motion and ruin your aim. This is something that improves with practice (lots). It is very common for your strikes to come up too short (you flexed your wrist or fingers), or too long (you moved your upper arm / wrist). Remember that you need to allow for the curvature of the hammerstone – it is hard to visualise hitting with a surface you cannot see!

Other than the action of the bicep / triceps, your upper arm should not move at all. Move through the motion of striking one more time in slow motion and be happy with your impact point.

Raise your arm and bring it down in a moderately fast 'whip' motion to strike the flint. All being well, the flint should produce a sharp 'crack' and a flake will detach. It may remain trapped under the flint nodule or land on the floor.

Put down the hammerstone and examine your handiwork. It can be really useful to take a flake and reattach it to the nodule / core. Study your impact point then detach the flake with your hand and turn it over. Check the bulb of percussion and any ripples, these are the signs of the travelling shockwave you created.

Don't be too disappointed with your first efforts, literally strike off a few flakes to get a feel for how the material reacts. We will be spending some time to refine these first attempts. Later in the book I will detail some common problems, their causes, and some solutions.

Safety reminder: get into the habit of always lifting your work piece after each strike. Clear away any debris, however small, and also abrade any sections of the nodule that are in contact with your hand. You may also need to abrade your working section, more on that later.
It's worth taking time to sift through any 'waste' material as you progress (wear gloves). Put aside any larger chunks that can be worked further. Discard any badly damaged chunks and any that exhibit inclusions. I like to separate my flakes into sizes and quality for further work.

15. Typical set-up.

16. Avoid or remove badly damaged areas.

17. Check strike point.

18. Detached flake after striking.

The next chapters will look at each of the main forms of knapping in detail. These are:

Direct percussion. Using hard hammers (stones) and introducing soft hammers (usually antler).

Indirect percussion. Once you get a real feel for flint and how it reacts, you might like to try this method. It uses another tool, usually a punch, along with a soft hammer to strike flakes.

Pressure flaking. Many tools can be simply struck flakes, that can be used 'as-is'. However, by using pressure flaking, we can further shape and refine flakes into more specific tools. As its name implies, this technique uses pressure rather than striking to remove material.

DIRECT PERCUSSION - CONTROLLED PRIMARY FLAKING

Hopefully you have now tried the very basics of knapping and started to understand a little of how the material reacts. It might seem an odd suggestion, but I found that starting with recreations of the simplest tools was very informative. If we travel back to the very beginning of the use of stone tools, we need to look to our more ancient ancestors – the Hominids. Over a quarter of a million years ago, these early proto-humans were creating simple but effective stone tools by striking flakes from pebbles to make simple 'choppers'. Making one is a great insight into the early beginnings of stone tool production and is a good introduction into knapping. Take a fist sized pebble and strike it with a hammerstone to take an angled flake from one 'end'.

Take a look at the diagram for guidance on angles and order of blows, two flakes opposing each other will make a more 'bladed' chopper. Rotating the piece through 90 degrees and repeating will create a very pointed chopper. Hopefully your strikes will each detach a flake and you will be left with a crude but effective tool. See pictures 19 - 20. Inverting the tool and holding it with the hand around the smooth end, it is easy to see how this could easily be used for hacking into bone, chopping through tendons, etc. when butchering an animal. Now pick up your detached flakes. If all went well each of them should be in one piece and have a very

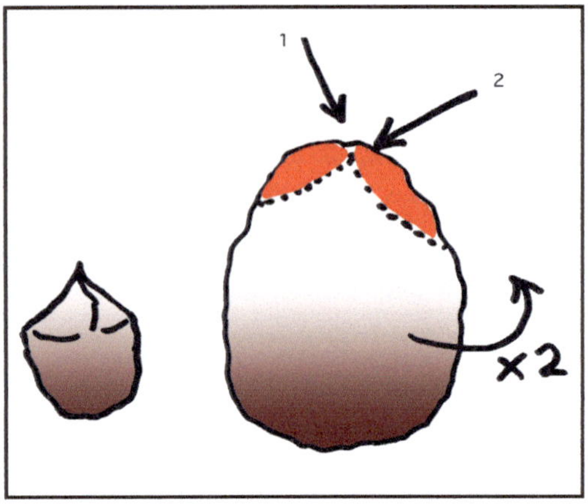

19. Take 2 or 4 flakes at 90 degrees to each other.

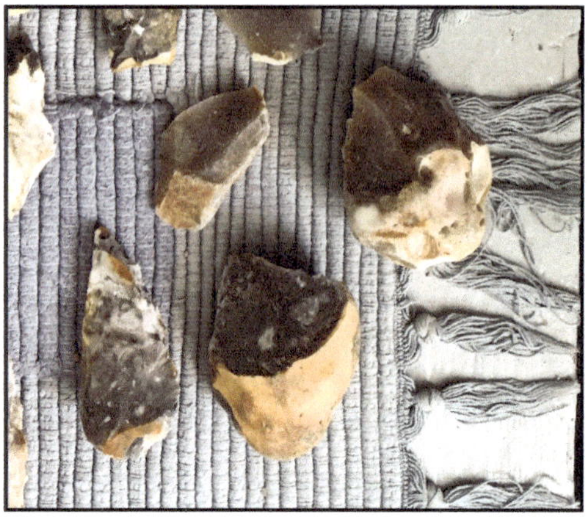

20. Beach flint 'choppers'.

sharp edge. These are instant-use tools that work well as small knives. This type of approach typifies some of the earliest tools created by man and are termed 'Oldowan' after the famous site of Olduvai Gorge in Africa.

Let's look at some more detailed theory before moving on to more challenging forms of knapping. There are some more 'rules' to observe in flint knapping, knowledge of which can help speed up the learning process and lead to smaller piles of waste flakes and frustration.

Once we gain access to the interior of the flint via basic quartering, things become perhaps more complicated. The point on the flint that you will strike is termed the platform and this needs to be the correct angle for a flake to detach successfully.

If the edge of the platform has faces that are over 90 degrees to each other, then no flaking will be possible, and any striking will just create damage via conical shock.

If the angles are close to 90 degrees, then the edge will invariably just crush.
If the edge 'falls' away at less than 90 degrees, then flaking will be possible. See picture 21 and example 3 as an ideal flake removal.

Picture 22 shows edge / platforms that show strike points and likely outcomes. Position 1 leads to a minimally invasive flake that may be too thin or is too close to the edge and may just crush. 2 is more ideal and

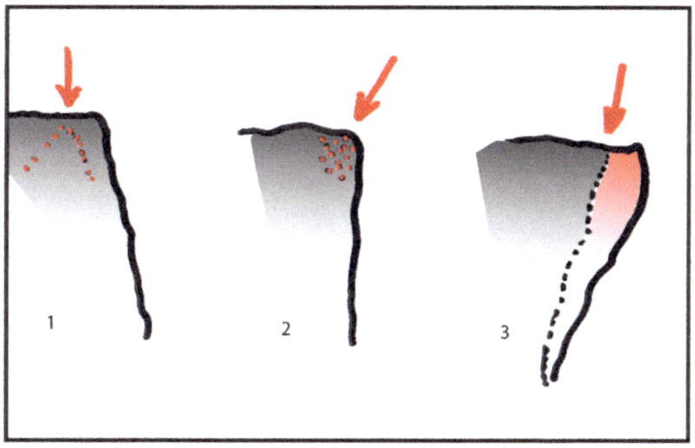

21. Over 90º, 2. 90º, 3. Under 90º.

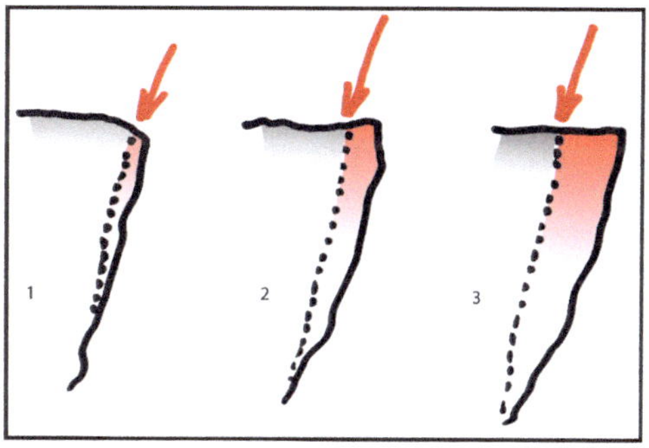

22. Increasingly invasive flakes.

leads to an ideal flake that tapers away nicely. 3 is very invasive and may remove too much material. This may have its uses, as we will see later on.

Here are the main types of flakes you will encounter (see picture 23).

1. The ideal flake that travels well into the material and then 'feathers' out to a very fine edge at the far (distal) end.

2. A 'hinged' flake. This is the product of not enough force / speed, the flake proceeds well but then ends quite abruptly with a thicker distal end.

3. A 'stepped' flake also proceeds quite well but then ends abruptly and even turns back on itself. This is caused by the shockwave hitting a flaw or internal damage in the flint.

4. An 'overshot' flake. This proceeds well but then carries on so far as to 'wrap' around the face of the flint, leading to an 'L' shaped flake. This is caused by excessive force / too invasive a strike point.

If you have enough material, keep taking successive flakes until most are nicely feathered and of good length and size. Along with the variables of material quality, your skill, etc. it will soon become obvious that angle of strike (along with position in from the edge) also play an important part. With care we can use the angle of strike / angle of the material to help us. See picture 24.

1. A steeper angle of attack, approaching the vertical, will lead to a very abrupt flake that will not travel very far into the material. This can be useful

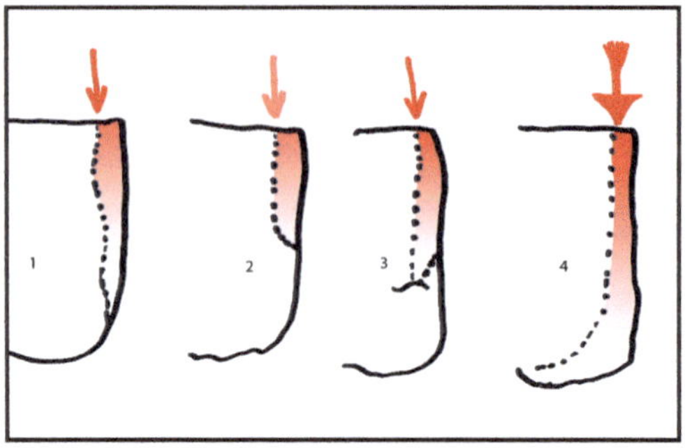

23. 1. Ideal, 2. Hinged, 3. Stepped, 4. Overshot.

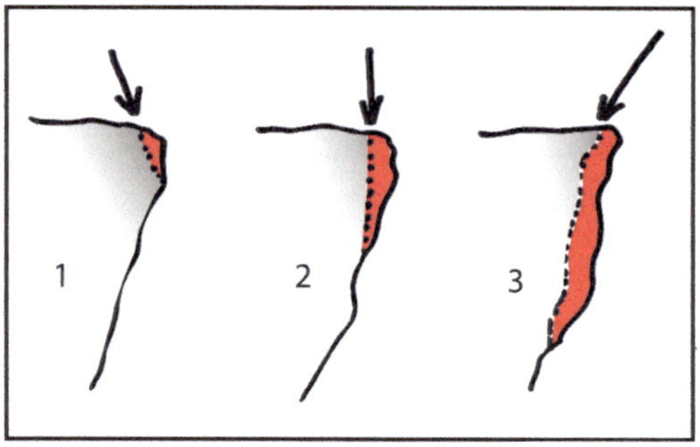

24. Changing angle of attack.

for platform preparation as we will see later on.

2. A vertical strike will lead to a more invasive flake that travels well into the material.

3. A shallower angle, aimed toward the bulk of the piece, coupled with more intrusive (further in from the edge) will lead to ever more invasive flakes that travel well across the material. This is the aim when we wish to rapidly thin down a piece of material.

We can combine the angle of the flint platform and the angle of attack to help when faced with trickier situations. If we have an edge whose angle is closer to 90 degrees, we have seen that a flake may not detach correctly. If we simply change the angle of the piece, as held on the leg, we can create an angle of attack that will fulfil the 'less than 90 degrees' rule. See picture 25.

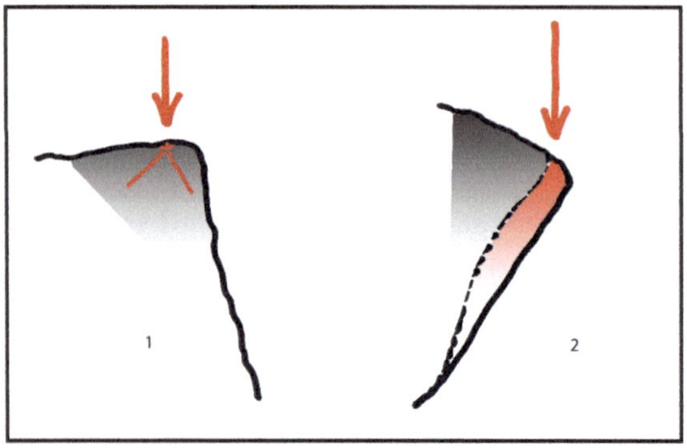

25. Over 90 degrees = failure.
Tipping the piece fulfils the less than 90 degree rule.

COMMON ERRORS

No flake. Not enough speed / force. Wrong angle. Striking too far into edge. Edge too steep.

Crushed platform. Too much force. Badly prepared platform. Wrong angle.

Flake too large. Striking too far into edge. Too much force / speed.

Flake too short. Striking too close to edge. Too little force / speed.

Flake too long. Too much force / speed. Wrong angle.

End shock (opposite end falling off). Any / all of the above issues, along with possible damage or inclusions inside the flint.

The solutions to nearly all these issues are, of course, study and more practice. Try to understand what went wrong and why, before trying again.

No flake. If you didn't succeed in removing a flake you may be able to increase speed / force and try again. If all variables are met, you will achieve a decent flake.

Crushed platform. You will have little choice but to strike slightly further into the material. Remove any loose material prior to doing this. If the damage is very bad you may need to flip the piece, remove an obtuse flake to remove the damaged area then try again from the other side.

Flake too large. You cannot put material back, no solution to this issue.

Flake too short. This should be easily remedied by taking further flakes.

Flake too long. The main problem with 'overshot' flakes is that they tend to 'wrap' around to another part of the work and this can have impacts on taking flakes from the area affected.

End shock. No solution. It can happen to even well-seasoned knappers. Either discard the pieces, glue them back together for a 'show' piece or try to make the parts into smaller tools.

If we follow the precedents set by our ancestors, we can now look at the two main choices they faced after basic quartering of a nodule. We can prepare the nodule and create a 'core', from which blades can be removed by striking or pressure, or we can use reduction flakes to thin the core into a 'preform' or 'roughout' – the beginnings of larger tools like hand axes.

CORE TOOLS / BIFACES

Let's look at core tools and introduce the concept of 'biface' technology.

A biface is simply a tool that has had flakes removed from both sides and is normally 'lentoid' (lens like) in section. Basically, it bulges out in the middle and has thin edges. Many types of tools and weapons fall into this category, from the instantly recognisable hand axes to spear and arrow points.

To create the typical lens profile of biface tools we need to understand the concept of what I call 'work and turn'. We will need to think several steps ahead. In fact, almost all flint knapping is improved by the ability to 'see' the finished tool inside the piece of flint you begin with. And then having the skills and knowledge needed to work your way through the material to liberate the finished item. If we need to remove thickness along one side, we will need to create a suitably large and stable platform from which to strike and create a flake removal.

The ability to create thinning flakes that travel at least halfway across the width of the piece we are working on will rely on careful preparation. See picture 26. If we take a more obtuse flake (1), we can then flip the piece over and see we have created a suitable platform from which to strike a longer thinning flake (2).

To expand on this further, I want to point out that this can seem quite confusing, and it sometimes seems counter to logical thinking. If our nodule has a raised area or thickness in the middle, we might think to take a flake from (3) but we actually make matters worse.

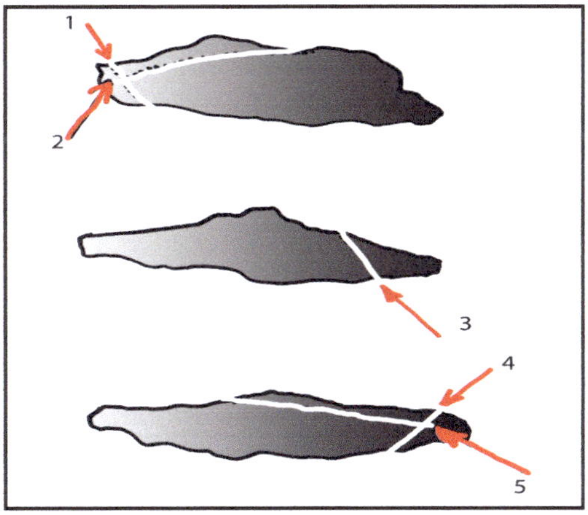

26. Bifacial thinning.

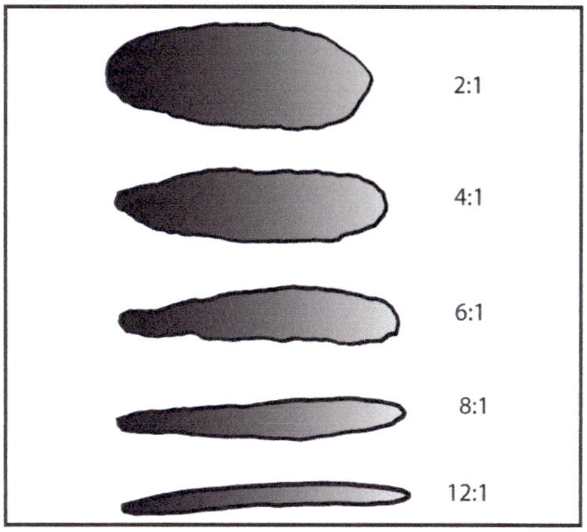

27. Thickness ratios.

What we need to do is take a flake from (4), turn the nodule over and use the resulting platform to strike (5) to create a flake that travels across the piece and removes the thickness as required.

If our goal is the ubiquitous hand axe (a Stone Age tool instantly recognised by all who see them), we need to remove material until we have a roughly circular shape that is thicker in the middle. We can achieve this by taking subsequent flakes around the edge, whilst repeatedly turning the piece over after each flake, to balance the edge with a flake from the opposite side.

Important note: As soon as we start taking flakes from a piece that requires turning around, it is very important that we take the time to abrade the edges that we are holding, or serious cuts can result. Usually, unless we are working on final flaking (which is some way off) we should get into the habit of strike / abrade. As soon as you have taken a successful flake we abrade that lovely sharp edge, both to render it safe for handling and to provide a stable platform for successive flakes. This can also seem counter intuitive like we are blunting our tool.

Using 'work and turn' we need to take flakes off all the way around and from both sides. This will result in a piece of flint with 'wavy' edges like a scallop shell. All the edges should then be abraded and be quite blunt. This preparatory work will have been achieved with a hammerstone but thinning flakes can be better achieved with a soft hammer, preferably a heavy antler tine or 'crown' end.

The goal now is to substantially reduce the thickness of the central area of the piece by using flakes that travel at least halfway across the work each time.

To achieve this successfully will need focus, skill and determination. The blows need to be accurate, invasive (in from the edge and at a suitable angle) and delivered with confidence. There is a good chance many of your early attempts will go awry but there is nothing more satisfying than landing a good blow and removing a successful thinning flake.

Once we have started to thin the biface we can give some attention to the final form. Most classic hand axes have a teardrop (Ogival) form. We need to remove more material from one end. This might be dictated by natural shaping or just choice. Leave one end more rounded and start to remove more material from the other end by using more abrupt flakes that bring the sides in to create a more pointed end. Some earlier types of hand axes even leave cortex on one end to act as a 'handle' area.

Hand axes varied greatly across time, with earlier examples being larger and thicker in section. Often cortex was left on at the 'hand' end and the 'business' end was more pointed. Later examples became smaller and more refined with thinner cross sections and a more oval perimeter.

Many flint knappers talk about the ratio of bifaces. They are referring to the cross-sectional thickness compared to the width of the piece. Earlier bifaces are closer to 4:1 or 6:1 (quite chunky) but later versions became ever thinner and approach 8:1 or even 10:1. This is very hard to accomplish and takes serious skill. There are very rare pieces that achieve an incredible 12:1 ratio that leaves them amazingly thin. see picture 27.

Another important concept to consider, especially with bifaces, is that of a centre line. Thinking back to our axe rough-out with the flaking all the way around, it created a wavy shell-like effect around the outer edge. If we look at this side on, we can see this wavy edge as it undulates up and down, picture 28. If we draw a line through all the low spots, we create a centre line. If we are trying to create thinning flakes we can only do so

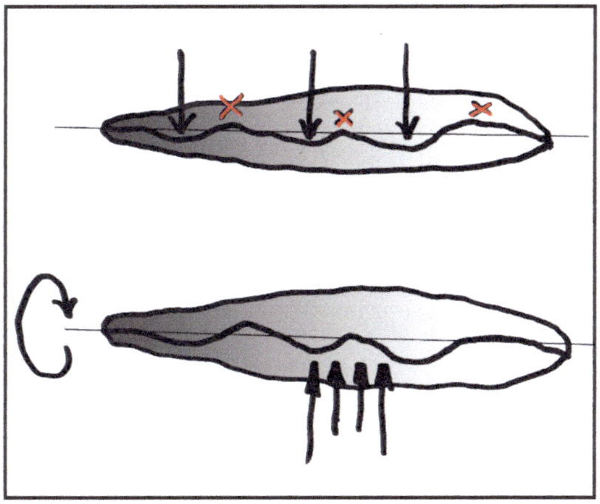

28. Centre line with platforms. Turning over and removing flakes will lower the high spots - see 29 for the result.

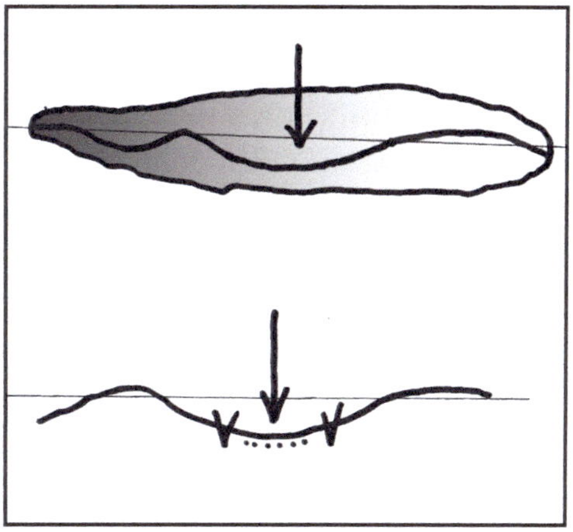

29. Small nibbles on either side of your platform help isolate it.

successfully if the platform we want to strike is below the centre line. If it is higher we need to bring it down below the centre before we can apply a thinning flake. This will require taking some small 'nibbled' abrupt flakes from the opposite side so flip the piece over to work on this area. This will lower the platform so that when we turn the piece back over, we have a new platform below the centre line once more. Knapping like this is worth doing slowly and carefully. No point rushing a strike and ruining all your previous work. See pictures 28 & 29. Picture 29 also shows the concept of taking tiny flakes from either side of a platform to aid it's release.

30. Lining up an antler hammer to remove a thinning flake.

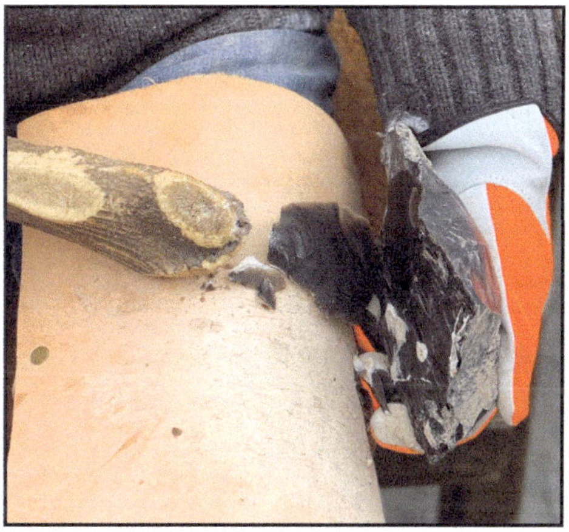

31. A succesful removal.

Study the faces of the flint piece you are working on and look at the areas you want to remove. Visualise that removal as a flake and then think about where the platform is located to create that flake. Turn the piece over and study the striking platform. Check its edge has it been abraded well, and does it look solid with no loose material? Hold the piece on your leather pad and line up your antler hammer. Check the angle of your flint, will your strike allow a shockwave to travel in the desired direction and at the desired depth? Place the hammer on the spot you are planning to strike and make a couple of slow-motion rehearsals of the full range of motion. On the last try, as you lift the hammer back up, suddenly reverse the

32.Thinning flake that displays nice parallel edges, ideal for a knife.

33. Flake removal scar.

direction into a whip-fast strike. Lift the work piece and study the result. Turn over the piece and replace the flake to really study it – how long is it, how wide, does it feather nicely? Each and every time you do this you will learn something new about flint and how it responds to being worked in this way. See pictures 30 - 37.

As your skills improve you will find that you are able to choose more suitable material. Faced with many shapes and sizes of flint nodules, you can start to visualise more clearly what might be coaxed out of each piece. By now you will probably have a good appreciation of just how wasteful most knapping is. We may need to remove up to 80% of a nodule to get to the 20% that can become a tool. As you encounter problems, or make mistakes, you will be faced with tough choices, to abandon the piece, or

34. Palm sized flake with thinning removals

35. Knapping in the hand with antler.

36. Section of cortex left on.

37. Other side showing flake scars, notice the two step fractures.

to correct the issue if possible and move forward. Some mistakes / problems like hinge or step fractures, intrusions, etc can be removed by striking an invasive flake that takes away the problem area. This may mean removing enough material from the opposite face to create a stable platform for the correcting flake removal. All this loses much material so solutions like this always come at a cost. I've found myself aiming for a nice large axe head, only to find that, in removing errors or problem areas, my axe reduces quite a bit in size!

Ultimately all knapping is like a 3D puzzle, where each choice of combination – angle / force of strike / choice of hammer, etc, all inform how we can proceed to the next step. Although I don't play, I imagine it is much like chess, thinking several moves ahead. It becomes a very cerebral exercise – finding or creating the next platform, striking and abrading. Take time to turn the work over and over in the hands. Really examine the angles, and potential problem areas. Think: removing that high spot will cost me some overall length, that strike failed so can I take another try? is that edge abraded enough? should I use a hard or soft hammer? etc.

Early on in my knapping efforts I found it very useful to try a range of strategies that can help, you might try some of these too:

Use a marker pen to put a spot on the flint where you intend to strike, and then check your accuracy after striking.

Make a card template showing a 100 degree angle to help visualise the likely path of a flake. Hold it against the side of your piece with the apex in line with your intended strike point. I also use a whiteboard to draw an outline of a typical nodule and then add a template over the top.
The template is drawn on clear acetate and is marked with the 100° angle. If I move this around on the whiteboard I can clearly visualise how points of contact and angles of the flint can affect the likely flake removal. See

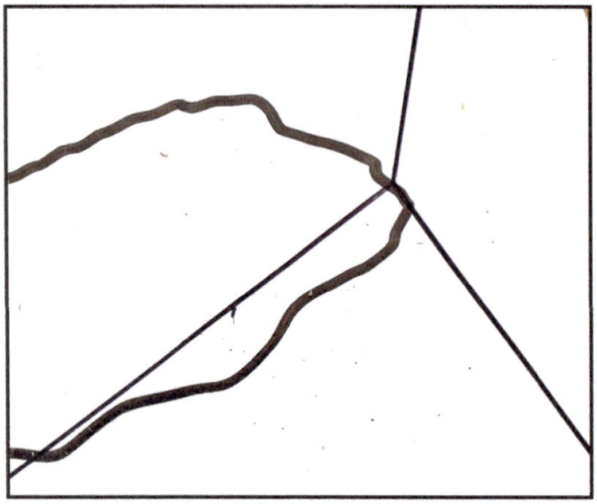

38. Acetate sheet with 100° marked over a whiteboard, on which I draw any shape of nodule.

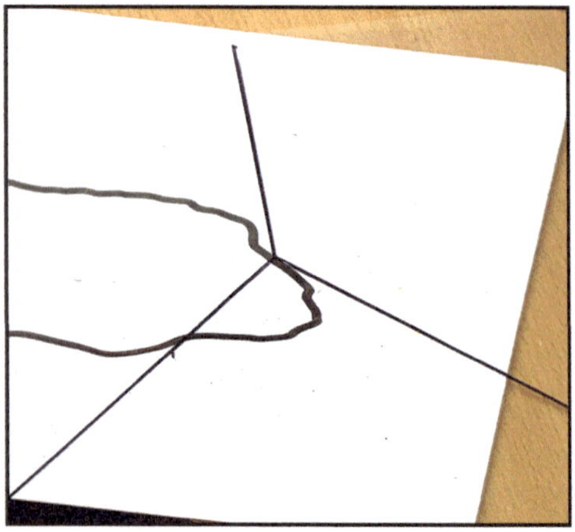

39. It allows me to visualise strikes and outcomes.

pictures 38 & 39.

Now let's take a moment to look at some keys issues in more detail. Picture 36 shows a biface 'rough-out'. I've marked some key areas.

1. Area of concavity. Ideally this wants to be close to the center line as visualised through the piece of flint. An area that lies on the center line should produce flakes that travel well into the piece. A platform below the center line is preferable for thinning flakes that may well travel right across the underside of the piece. If your striking area is too far above the center line any flakes may be pulled short or break.

2. The strike point. This is where your antler billet will make contact so it's important that it is abraded and solid with no intrusions or tiny flaws. Abrading is important here to create a solid edge to transmit thshockwave

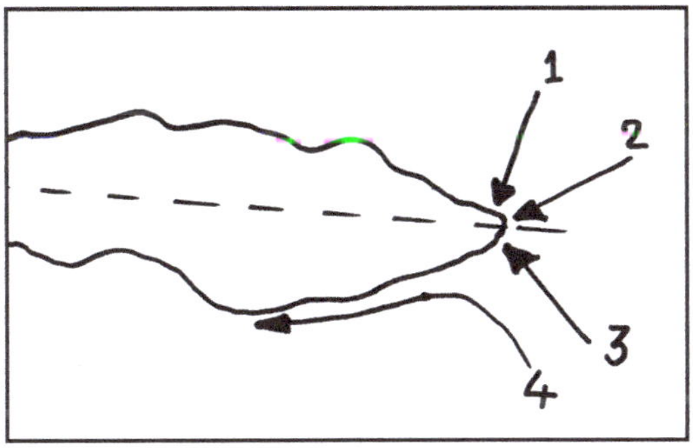

40. Platform geometry.

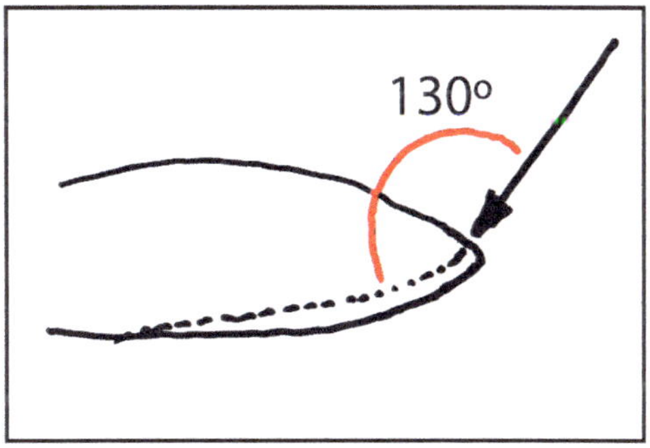

41. Flake removal - 130° from strike.

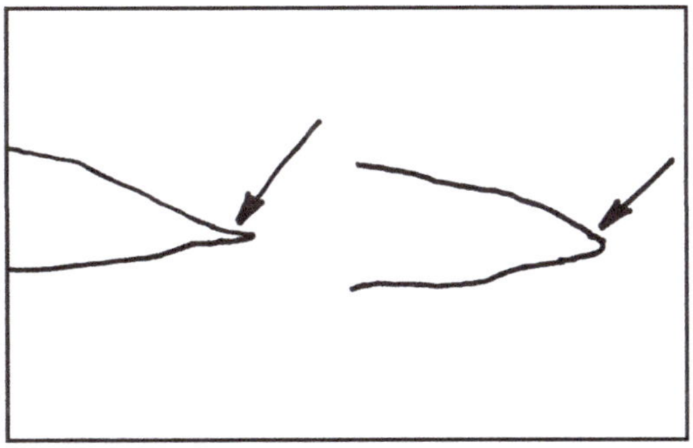

42. Edge too thin (left). Abraded and sound (right).

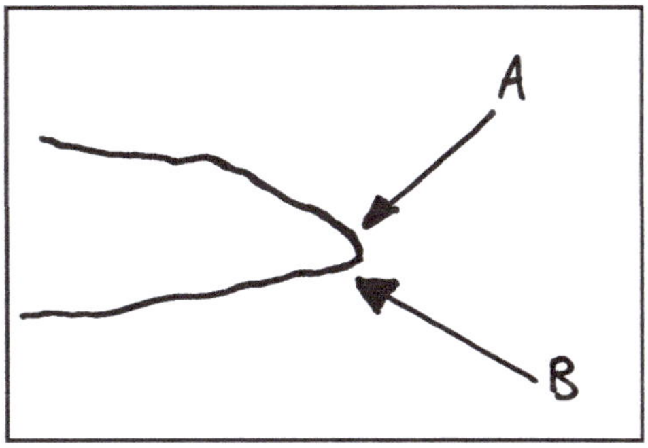

43. Angled 'bevel'.

into the piece and detach a succesful flake. Don't abrade up and down (vertically to the working edge) as this will destroy the striking platforms geometry. Make sure you abrade horizontally and not too much.

3. The underside of your platform. This should ideally be more or less convex or bulge down. We don't want any concavity under here. We need a reasonable thickness of material to help the shockwave travel. Any areas of damage will severely shorten or stop flake propagation.

4. The flake 'pathway'. The area you are hoping to remove with the struck flake. If you already have flake removal scars then any new flake will try to travel underneath any ridges so keep this in mind when setting up any removals. If the area is uniformly thicker then flakes should travel well. Any areas of damage or that have inclusions will hamper clean flake production and you should be looking to undercut them. You will need a well prepared platform and a solid accurate strike to travel through difficult areas.

Picture 41 shows how flakes will try to travel at 130° from the angle of strike. Do not confuse this with the 100° hertzian cone that intiates the flakes removal.

Picture 42 shows how platform edge must not be too thin. Remove small abrupt flakes and / or abrade to create a good stable edge.

Picture 43 shows how the edge needs to have an angled 'bevel' right where you will strike. This will need to point down at around 45° - 60°. If this angle is too low / shallow then the edge is likely to collapse. Too steep and your blow may just glance off with no flake removal. If you don't cause too much damage you may be able to adjust the bevel angle with careful abrading before trying again.

All of this will take time to experience and control. Use any larger waste flakes you have created to practice your aim and try taking a range of short and longer flakes by changing angles of attack / bevel /abrasion, etc. If a piece of flint turns out to have lots of flaws or intrusions don't feel bad about discarding it and trying a fresh piece.

Let's follow a typical session: I often decide what to make once I've seen how a particular piece of flint reacts and what kind of flakes I achieve. In this case a nodule was selected that was slightly longer and with some thickness to one end. I took an initial flake and the flint looked OK. I then started taking flakes that were minimally invasive. The goal is to start to remove any troublesome areas, cortex and to provide a scar that becomes a suitable platform for the next flake. Flake, flip over, abrade then flake. This should lead to a nice zig-zag or wavy edge. See pictures 40 - 44.

Occasionally, if you have set things up well - good platforms, well abraded, etc. then you may achieve an ideal flake removal as shown in pic. The next strike and all my good luck vanished! My strike was a little over-powered and it caused end shock - my nodule broke in half. This happens often enough that one just needs to shrug and move on. Maybe with greater skill I could have avoided it but this problem affects all knappers so best just look at how you can recover the situation. I chose to use the rather flat surface to strike flakes as from a core. See pictures 52 & 53.

It was disappointing but I still managed to get some good material for other projects. That large flake was turned into a knife and many of my removal flakes became scrapers and small tools.

44. Nodule selected and studied.

45. I took this first flake and flint looked OK.

46. I moved to the other end and took a couple of flakes.

47. Another nice flake.

48. Working around the edge.

49. A nice intrusive strike.

50. The ideal removal.

51. Then my luck changed.

52. Preparing to strike a flake from a core.

53. The struck flake. We can rotate the core and keep taking flakes all the way around.

A side note on abrading. As previously mentioned, abrading edges is an important part of the knapping process and one that is best not to skip.

54. Abrading a platform.

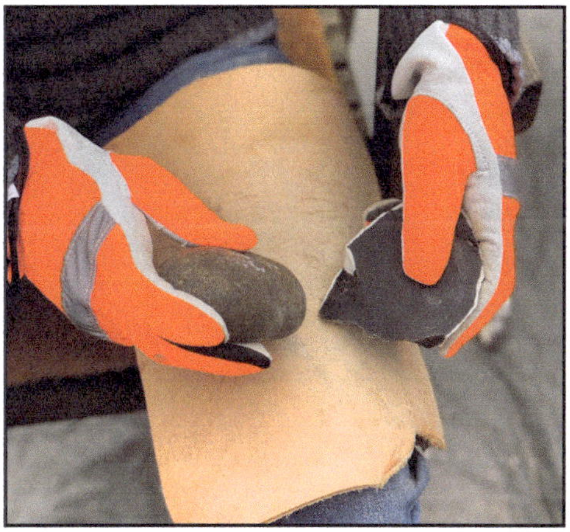

55. Ready to strike abraded platform.

Using an abrasive stone, rub horizontally along any edge to create a suitable and stable platform. Avoid rubbing vertically down the face of the edge as this will change it's geometry too much. As you become more experienced you may wish to do this to remover more material more quickly if you need to further consolidate an edge platform. It becomes a cross between abrading and edge knapping.

PRESSURE FLAKING

Pressure flaking uses a suitable tool to detach a flake using pressure, rather than percussion (striking). As you might imagine this takes some considerable force, but we can make life easier for ourselves by adopting certain tactics.

Hopefully you have been practicing your primary flaking (via percussion) and have made a pile of flakes. Choose one a bit smaller than your palm, and not too thick, to practice on.

56. Hand position for pressure flaking.

57. Intrusive flakes - push IN towards opposite edge THEN downwards flex.

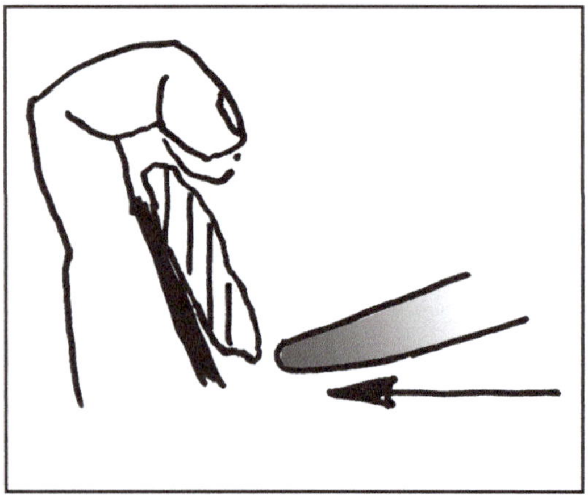

58. Abrupt flakes to create a strong edge.

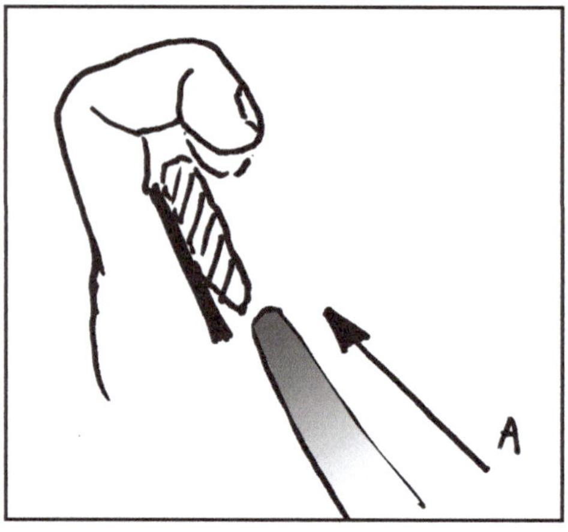

59. Intrusive flakes - push IN towards opposite edge THEN downwards flex.

You will need a small but thick leather pad and an antler tine, using the pointed end of the antler. Rather than hitting the flint, we will be using a pushing force to detach small flakes. Hold the flint piece on small leather pad, in your left hand, and curl your fingers over so all your fingertips are resting on top of the flint flake. Turn your hand over so that your fingernails are upper and pointing towards you. You may turn your hand down slightly, so thumb is uppermost, see picture 56. Holding the antler, or copper tipped flaker as I'm using, firmly in the other hand. Apply the pointed end to the edge of the flint, at an approximately 30 degree angle. You may need to flex your left hand away from your body to help achieve

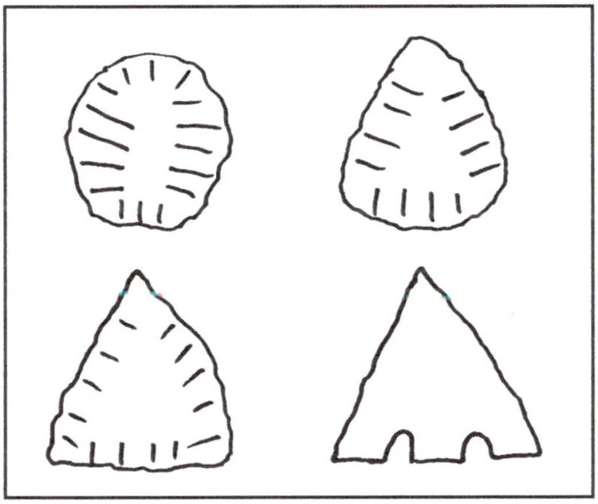

60. Working inwards from three directions.

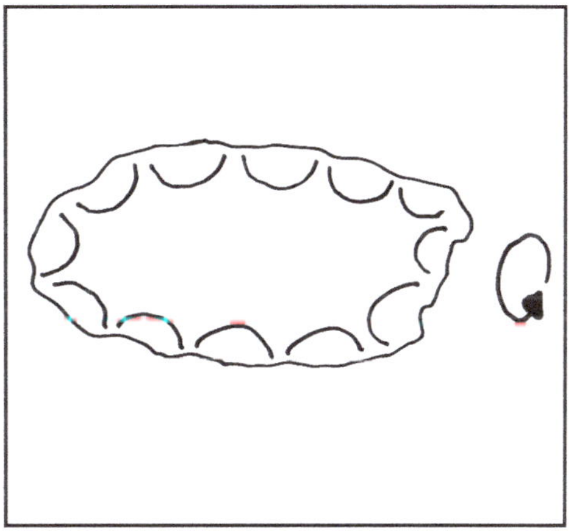

61. Flakes scars all around edge then flip and repeat.

62. Working down one edge.

63. The finished 'leaf' arrow head.

the right angle. You are looking to push inwards firmly – aim towards the knuckles on your left hand. You can rest the back of your left hand against the inside of your knee for support. Push in very firmly with the antler tine and then flex downwards, towards the palm of the hand, see picture 51. This should cause a flake to detach from the work piece with a solid 'click'. If you find this hard (it is) use your right knee to push the hand with the antler – like closing your knees together. Or even try flexing both legs inwards as this brings the workpiece and the antler together. With practice this can provide powerful force into the antler and the flint edge. Clear off any loose material before further work. Abrade the edges as you go with a rough stone abrader. Work round the piece of flint in a roughly circular direction. You will need to flip the flint over regularly and work from the other side too. You are aiming for flakes that are invasive and travel a good way across your flint flake. If they are coming up a bit short you will need to change your angle of attack and / or provide more force. It can help to take more abrupt flakes as these create a strong platform, from which it is easier to create longer flakes. Intrusive flakes should travel well into the shape - push INWARDS and then flex DOWNWARDS. This can take a while to get to grips with. Remember to abrade often to create stable platforms or the edge will just crush.

Once your flint is both thinner and rounder, start working from only three directions / 'sides' and start to push the shape into more of a triangle. See pictures 60 - 61. With patience, effort and some luck you will end up with a triangular arrow point with serrated edges. Bottom right shape in pic 60 will be explained a little later.

If you can source thick glass or ceramics, you can approach it in the same way you would flint and use all methods of flake removal. Modern glass replicas of ancient tools like hand axes have a surprising beauty. In the last two centuries Aboriginal Australians quickly adapted to creating very effective arrow and spear points from discarded glass bottles.

To try this, select a bottle with a flatter bottom and not too thick. Coloured bottles work best as it's easier to see what you are doing to them – green or brown. To get the bottom off, put a large steel nail (4") point down into the clean and dry bottle. Wear eye protection and gloves and work outside. Put your thumb over the top of the bottle and shake vigorously up and down. After much shaking the bottom should just pop off, so ensure

64. Insert nail or screw point down.

65. Allow bottom to fall off onto cloth.

66. Working around the edge to create a flatter surface and start flake scars.

67. Nice and circular with scars all the way around the edge.

68. Press firmly in on the edge then flex down to hear a sharp click.

69. Flake scars that travel a good way across the other side.

70. Flake scars on a prepared 'blank', ready for further shaping.

71. Finished small leaf arrowhead.

it has something soft to land on. See pictures 64 - 65. Dispose of the bottle and any shards very carefully. Now fully abrade all around the edge. You can now carefully use this in place of a flint piece. I use a large antler tine as a kind of 'anvil' to help start the edge flaking. Using a smaller tine I take quite small abrupt edge flakes, rotating the glass until I've gone all the way around. See pictures 66 - 67.

Once I've gone all the way around one side I flip the piece over and check the flake scars which should look like picture 69. Abrade the edge all the way around and then go again but starting from this newly scarred side to throw flakes into the other face. You will need to repeat this process a few times, flipping the piece and abrading each time. Start to nibble a bit more from two of the 'sides'of the circle to push it into a more oval shape. If you progress slowly and carefully you should be rewarded with a pleasing 'leaf-shaped' arrow head. See picture 71.

Notching

Once you have made a few leaf or basic triangular shaped arrow heads you might be ready for a more challenging style. Flint didn't drop out of favour completely when metal came along in the form of copper and then bronze. Right into the Bronze Age flint was still being used and the arrow heads developed into a new style that I think is rather beautiful. Called 'barbed and tanged', these arrow heads are a broad based triangle that then has small notches encroaching into the bottom edge. Two notches

72. Triangle shaped arrowhead ready for notching.

73. Position antler tine / copper flaker carefully and take tiny flakes.

separate the bottom edge into a central 'tang' that is fitted into a long thin haft or arrow shaft. The two outer lobes then hang down on either side. This increases the width of the arrow and also makes it less likely to fall out of any animal that it has been shot into.

To create these we will need to start with a nicely even flake about 8x8cm and not too thick. Using all the same techniques we learnt with the leaf arrows, we need to work our way around the edge and then start to push inwards from three directions to create a more triangular shape. Refer

74. Progressing slowly into the notch.

75. Finished notched arrowhead.

back to picture 60. Remember, abrupt flakes all the way around on both sides, abrade to consolidate edge, then inwards pressure to push long flakes. Once you have a nice clean triangle we can look at adding the notches. The trick or rather skill to this process is go slowly. Aim to remove only tiny flakes each time. You will need a slim ended antler tine or a flatter copper flaker. You can use a short flat-bladed screwdriver but steel can be a bit harsh and is more likely to causes breakages.

Start by marking two equidistant points on what will become your bottom edge. Using a steeper angle (refer back to pic. 54) take a very small flake from the edge. Flip over and repeat from the other side. Once you have progressed a few millimetres into the flint do the same thing on the second mark to make the next notch. We don't want to throw longer flakes for these as we don't want scars, just keep 'nibbling' away at the notches so that they progress into the flint. Once you are about 5mm in you will need to use a flatter tool. It becomes important that only the very end of the tool presses on the inside end of the notch, and NOT the sides of the notch. Any pressure on the sides is a sure way to break off your tang (or barbs). Progress slowly and make sure the flint arrow is well supported underneath at all times. I use a doubled over piece of thinner leather or a piece of flat rubber sheet. If you use a flatter tool you can try a gentle rocking motion to detach the flakes - push down onto the edge at the inside end of the notch and then rock the tool towards the direction of the notch. Expect to break a few as you learn this new skill. The key things to remember are to go slowly and to support the piece well from underneath. Once you get better at these it can be very satisfying as they are a wonderfully pleasing shape - a bit of a flint classic. Refer to 72 - 75.

CORE PREPARATION FOR FLAKE TOOLS

Sometimes, after quartering a nodule, you may end up with a medium sized piece with a flatter top of exposed flint, and a rounded cortex covered bottom. Pictures 76 - 77 show taking a typically 'bulbous' protrusion from a large nodule preparing the edge for flaking. With a little careful processing we can turn this into a 'blade core'. Let's start by abrading well all around the top edge to give a nice stable platform for striking. Lay the nodule of your leg pad and, using a soft hammer, strike a little into the edge. Aim for the angles needed to create an invasive flake that, hopefully, will travel the length of the nodule. Abrade again and repeat a little way from your previous removal. At this point it will be worth switching to an indirect method that uses a punch as it greatly increases

76. Nice bulbous protrusion from a nodule.

77. Bulbous section struck off and edge prepared.

accuracy. It can be helpful to isolate each removal by taking some very small flakes from either side of our striking point. This can be achieved with a pressure flaker, preferably a copper-tipped one. With more abrading our platform should now stick out like the prow on a tiny ship. This will improve our chances of isolating a section when flaking.

The easiest way to use a punch is to grip the core between your knees, leaning it so that the side that will be worked upon is lowest – nearer to the right knee. Make sure your leather pad covers the top and side of the leg next to the area that will be struck. For safety it is sensible to also place some padding on the inside of the left knee and make sure there are no sharp edges on the sides or bottom of the core. Hold the punch in your

78. Antler hammer and punch for striking blades.

79. A blade after release.

left hand and locate the tip onto the top edge of the flint core that is nearest your right knee, about 4mm in from the edge. Check your angles and, using a hammerstone or a wooden mallet, strike the top of the punch with a sharp rap. All being well you should get a nice blade removal. Too little speed / force will result in a shorter blade, whilst too much may even wrap under the core (overshot fracture). As you are holding the core gripped between the knees you will need to gently release and catch both the core and the released flake to study your handiwork. See pictures 78 - 79.

80. Another blade, working our way around the core.

81. A selection of blades struck and some smaller cores.

82. Antler hammer and 'anvil' for edge re-touching

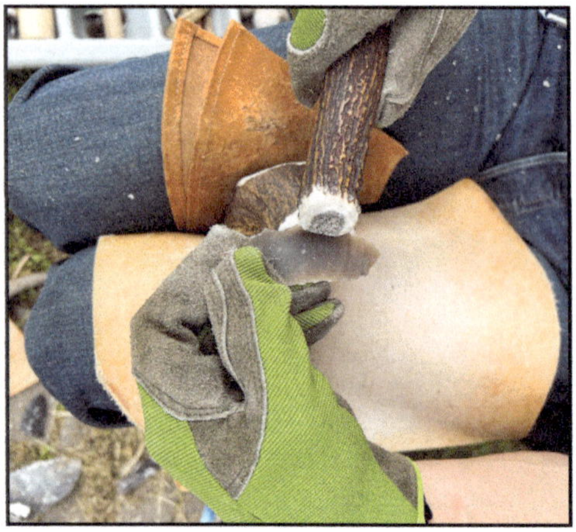

83. Working along an edge, either to blunt it or to consolidate a cutting edge.

84. Notching into one edge of a flake blade.

85. Snap blade at notch point.

We will work our way around the core like this. Once we are back at our start point, we can now start removing flakes that, if successful, will have the crest scars of the previous removals running down the length of the blades. This can take some time to get the hang of but eventually you will have the satisfaction of creating longer blades with nice parallel sides that are amazingly sharp, time after time. In theory we can keep repeating this until the parent core shrinks down and becomes smaller and smaller, with the resulting blades also decreasing in size.

Flakes / blades created in this way will be extremely sharp and can be used for a wide variety of tasks. If you plan to actually use any it is

86. Abrupt flaking along one edge to form an angle.

87. A selection of Mesolithic style flakes.

advisable to heavily abrade or run abrupt retouch along one edge, so that is safely blunt for holding. Even the 'blade' edge can be retouched slightly as it makes a stronger and more stable cutting edge. See pictures 82 and 83.

Taking some smaller blades, if we pressure flake a small notch at some point along the length of the blade, we can use this as a weakness to break the blade into smaller sections. This can liberate several tools from just one flake blade. This was the approach used in the Mesolithic (Middle Stone Age). It is thought this may have been to preserve resources; a core could be carried around and fashioned into many types of tools. Some of these tools / blades (microliths) are so small that to be useful they need to be hafted with several in a row to create a longer cutting edge. The cores were often used until they ended up being just 20-40mm high. See 84 - 87.

'EVERYDAY' KNAPPING

It is satisfying to set out with a goal to make a specific tool, say a hand axe, however early on many frustrations and failures may be met. An alternate strategy is to start with primary flaking, using a hard hammer, and see what flakes and shapes emerge. If a pleasing flake is removed, you could pause and take a look at it. A well feathered flake is a tool in its own right, but perhaps we can alter or improve it? I personally believe that our ancestors, although very skilled, must have also made mistakes or been surprised by faults within their chosen material. It seems likely that they will have used the resulting pieces, rather than discarding them. Different shape flakes lend themselves to different types of tools and uses so I often just start knapping and see what transpires. Once I've created a few good flakes I tend to stop and look at them to see what they might become.

If I have a smaller, but thicker, flake I might consider that if very abrupt flakes are removed all around the edge, we may encourage it into a more circular shape with a steeper edge. This is the shape favoured in the past for scraping, probably in animal hide preparation. So called 'scrapers' vary in size and shape but are usually fairly flat on the underside with a steep sided edge created by abrupt secondary flaking. Sometimes this is all the way around the shape. The idea being that this allowed them to be 'pushed' along the inside of an animal skin / hide to remove fat. As some ancient examples are very small (25mm or less) it is my belief that many must have been hafted (fitted to handles) for use.

Flakes with pronounced irregular edges or 'sticky-out' bits might be coaxed into borers / piercers or burins - tools for piercing various materials, from hide to wood and antler. Google names if you want to check the wide variety of shapes created by our ancestors.

Flakes of a larger size that have more parallel edges can become knives, abraded or abruptly retouched on one edge to make is easier to hold. Similar flakes may be made into sawing tools by using a pressure flaker to create regular small removals along one edge. This creates a tooth-like or denticulate profile that will saw through wood, bone and antler very efficiently.

88. Various tools: Ovate handaxes, scrapers, blades, knives. Inset - a large denticulate 'saw'.

89. 'Fabricator' or strike-a-light. 10cm long and made on a triangle section.

90. Very large oval handaxe of the type used by Neanderthals. 18cm.

91. Acheulian style handaxe.17cm

92. Small axe head.12cm.

93. Solutrean spear point.12cm.

94. Discoidal knife. 9cm.

Mid-sized flakes that are not too thick, and are quite even, make good contenders for pressure flaking into arrow heads. Slightly larger ones are ideal for spear points.

Larger flakes or smaller rough-outs that suffer damage to one edge, perhaps on overly invasive flake or a mis-judged impact point, can be turned into hollow-edged scrapers. These were probably used for shaving wood (and other materials), the obvious use being straightening arrow or spear shafts. The following pictures show a selection of my work where I was just testing my slowly growing skills and seeing what would appear. A keen eye will spot the odd mistake or flaw, but I managed a range from discoid 'knives' to scrapers and a small hand axe.

PROBLEM SOLVING

Dealing with various issues that arise whilst flint knapping is one of the things that takes time to learn. Approach each issue as a learning opportunity and if the solution doesn't work out then keep trying until you succeed. Very often you will be faced with damaged areas or inclusions in the piece of flint you are working on. The only way to push past them is to carefully plan and prepare the best platform you can create. Often you will need a deep and very invasive flake that travels past the area of issue. Fossil inclusions and chalky cortex may well be much deeper than any surface indications and will need a robust flake that undercuts them

95. Problem area with chalk and holes.

96. Successful removal of complete area.

fully.

Recently I was working on a piece that had a large section of chalk in the form of 'holes' that often occur in flint nodules. I dug around with a tine and could see some of it was pretty deep. Just to make matters worse, the same area was very lumpy and uneven with some signs of surface damage. All in all quite a challenge. Looking at how far my flake would need to travel I turned the piece over and took a solid but shorter flake to create a good sized platform. I then abraded the edge well and checked my angles. To help the flake travel well I used a heavy section of crown antler. A solid whack caused the whole section to shatter. Not an ideal outcome but all the problem areas were removed so I took it as a win and a sign that the area was even more damaged than I thought. See pictures 95 - 96.

Refer to the section on common errors often. As you encounter issues take a look and see if you can identify what went wrong and think about how you would have approached the work differently. Perhaps the platform was ill prepared or your strike was not accurate enough? Are you using the right tool for the job? Working with whatever flint you have will force you to deal with all these issues and many more. 'Perfect' flint doesn't exist but when you find any that is nice and black with very few inclusions you may find that things start to go well and follow the 'rules' that you have learnt. Flint with lots of inclusions is very challenging but can teach you much about the process. Always give yourself plenty of time to look over the flint and plan your next move. Think over the angles of attack, edge preparation, amount of force needed, etc. before every strike. As you gain experience this process will become quicker and eventually intuitive. I find that looking at the result of any strike, and comparing it with my imagining outcome, teaches me much about the process.

Key points to remember are: you need a concave or thinning section to initiate flake removal. The edge needs to be sufficiently strong to propogate the shockwave so abrade correctly. Flint likes to follow ridges so use this to your advantage. Use a well aimed strike of sufficent force to detach the flake you are trying for.

97. Scraper.

98. Handle for scraper.

99. Small spear and arrow.

100. Micro-lith arrow and knife.

HAFTING

This refers to the fitting of a tool to a 'handle'. As very few ancient examples of hafted tools remain, there is much conjecture over which tools were hafted and how. Trying to use replicas of tools whose shapes dictate probable uses, quickly makes it apparent that many are more efficient or comfortable to use when fitted to a handle. If your goal is to make display or demonstration pieces (especially if you plan to use them), then you may wish to haft them. Unless you need to be strictly 'historically accurate' (constrained by lack of evidence) then you can reasonably fit whatever handle seems expedient to the end use. There is enough historical evidence to show that many materials were used for hafting;

antler, bone, and wood being the main ones.

Hand tools usually just need some kind of cylindrical shaft that extends the tool and allows it to be more easily grasped. This cylinder then has cuts fashioned into it to allow the flint tool to be partially inserted. The tool can be held in place with natural cordage (string), animal sinew (tendon) and / or glue, and often a combination of cordage and glue. You may need to take some abrupt flakes from the end of the flint to allow it to fit the handle more easily. The thinner section sticking out the back of a 'knife', for example, is called a tang. 'Stone Age' glue was created from a mix of tree resin (often pine), beeswax and crushed charcoal. This mix can be applied in a molten state and quickly dries to a semi-rigid but tacky consistency.

I will not cover the creation of this mix in any detail here, but internet searches will reveal more information and pictures / videos. I often sell materials like pine glue via my Etsy store. See pictures 97 - 100 for some example hafting projects.

MODERN TOOLS / MODERN MATERIALS

Flint knapping has quite a following in the Americas, and they have adapted many tools to use modern materials. Rather than hammer stones or antler hammers they often use 'copper boppers', wooden cylinders weighted with lead and faced with copper. Pressure flaking tools are made from durable materials like Delrin (hard wearing plastic) or hardwood, with copper or brass inserts. Quite an industry has arisen to fashion replicas of the kind of tools made by ancient Indigenous Americans, but also more creative pieces that don't follow any ancient tradition. To this end, many types of equipment have been fashioned that may help with laborious pressure knapping – 'jigs' and platforms that hold the work piece and help to exert the forces required. Although many knappers in the US are proficient at primary knapping via percussion, there is also a huge following of folks that use prepared 'slabs' – flat preforms that are shaped further via pressure flaking only. You will find further information via many of the US knapping groups that can be found online.

As mentioned, some thicker ceramics and tiles can be knapped but they are mostly much softer than flint so you will need adapt your technique accordingly. Some thicker floor tiles are quite cheap so practice does not carry a prohibitive cost. See the pictures below for some examples and a short sequence on knapping a floor tile to create a biface tool.

101. Modern tools - nylon and copper.

102. Copper billet used to knap a thick ceramic flooring tile.

103. Edge removal on a tile.

104. Biface preparations on tile.

SUMMING UP

There are so many more things I could have covered as the use of flint is a huge subject. I definitely recommend looking up illustrations and catalogues of the many types of tools known, or even better, go and visit a museum and see the real things. Any chance you get to look at sources like these can help you to be a better knapper. Study and try to decipher how the tool was created, and how you might achieve a similar item.

There is much satisfaction to be had if you actually try to use any of the tools you create. Whether it is within ancient re-enacting, education, bushcraft or other spheres. It gives solid glimpses into the mindset of our ancient ancestors. I suggest there is a good degree of latitude when it comes to authenticity as much is not known, or certain. Experimental Archaeology, where different methods and approaches are tried to help discover which ones are most productive / likely, has helped inform what we know of ancient tools and their likely uses. For example, trying to use smaller tools proves to be quite fiddly and it seems quite logical that these were hafted for use. I have taken smaller blade flakes, inserted them into a hole created in a small section of tree branch 'handle' and then used this as a very efficient 'spoke shave' that shaves down wood just as well as any modern steel tool. Often scrapers will feature a small bump at the rear of the scraping surface that could well be were a wooden haft was attached. I've made replicas like this and they work very well.

Towards the end of the main use of flint tools, in the Neolithic, biface axes were sometimes polished. This is very hard to accomplish as flint is so hard. The evidence points to the use of slabs of very abrasive stones like limestone or granite, along with sand and water. It can take many hundreds of hours of very physical rubbing work to smooth the outside of a knapped axe. The results, however, can be amazingly beautiful. We are unsure whether these axes were used or just pretty status symbols but there is evidence that smoothing in this way makes them last longer in use as the stresses are allowed to flow more evenly though the material. I know of only a few people in the UK who have taken the time to complete this process.

I sincerely hope that this book has helped you start, or even improve, your flint knapping skills. Do feel free to contact me with stories of success, you'll find my info in the Resources section. It should come as no surprise that it can take many hours (hundreds) to have any real control over outcomes when flint knapping and real mastery make take 1,000 hours. I consider I have plenty of scope for future learning myself. I have been lucky to be able to attend workshops by some very accomplished knappers in the UK and have I learned much from these experiences, I encourage you to do the same. I often offer workshops or 1-2-1 sessions so look up my contacts at the end of this book. In recent years there has been a resurgence in interest in ancient crafts and skills (in the UK) so you may find courses offered via living history museums, craft centres, outdoor skills and bushcraft learning facilities.

105. Real flint artifacts with typical surface 'patina' as found in UK field walking.

RESOURCES AND MATERIALS

Etsy. This e-store site has plenty of resources from flint, tools, antler, and knapped flint tools. I sell a range of knapping kits and tools, along with reproductions on my own Etsy store, which can be found at: https://www.etsy.com/uk/shop/JonnyCraftsThings

Google search 'Flint suppliers' for merchants selling rough building flint nodules.There is no denying that, whatever we might think about social media it can be a useful place to find and share information. You will find informative videos on YouTube, groups devoted to flint knapping on Facebook, examples of modern and ancient knapping on Instagram, etc. Throughout all there is a bias towards the Americas, but UK style knapping is well represented if you search.

FURTHER READING

Prehistoric Flintwork, Chris Butler. A very thorough overview of the many types of tools and flint artefacts that can be found in the UK. Aimed primarily at identification for Archaeologists, it is an excellent source for the aspiring flint knapper with great illustrations of the wide variety of tools that can be fashioned from flint.

The Nature and Subsequent Uses of Flint, John Lord. A great introduction to flint knapping. Sadly, it is out of print so look out for second hand copies.

Flint Knapping, Robert Turner. A solid book with great information. Also covers the modern tradition of flint tools as found in the Americas.

Man the Tool-maker, K.P. Oakley. A good review of tool-making traditions around the world. Out of print so look for second hand.

Ice Age Britain, N. Barton. Lots of interesting information about the early peoples in Britain (and UK) and the tools they made.

A free PDF on flint tool identification (in the UK) is available from Leicester University:
https://leicsfieldworkers.files.wordpress.com/2021/03/flint_id_guide.pdf

COURSES & DEMONSTRATIONS

As previously stated, one of the best ways to learn more about knapping is to attend a course run by an experienced knapper. You will find excellent courses offered by Will Lord and Butser Ancient Farm in Wiltshire, amongst others.

I offer practical workshops and knapping demonstrations. I'm based in NW London and can be contacted at jonnycope@hotmail.com

ACKNOWLEDGMENTS

I would like to thank my wife Rosy for help in editing and proof-reading the text, and my son Charlie for many of the photographs. I learned much, early on in my journey, from workshops with Will Lord and James Dilley. I would also like to thank the land owners and farmers who have let me remove flint from their fields.